In Praise of Usefulness

Also by Angela Patten

Reliquaries

Still Listening

High Tea at a Low Table

In Praise of Usefulness

—POETRY—

ANGELA PATTEN

Maple Tree Editions
An Imprint of Onion River Press
191 Bank Street
Burlington Vermont 05401

For Daniel

In Praise of Usefulness
Poetry
Copyright 2014 by Angela Patten

All rights reserved. No part of this book may be used or reproduced in any manner whatsoever without written permission except in the case of brief quotations embodied in critical articles and reviews.

Cover and book design by Laurie Thomas
Cover photo by Craig Thomas

ISBN: 978-1-949066-02-9

Published by Maple Tree Editions, an Imprint of Onion River Press
191 Bank Street, Burlington, Vermont, USA

(Originally published by Wind Ridge Books in 2014, ISBN: 9781935922568)

Contents

Acknowledgements ix

PART I

Tabula Rasa 3
Always Room for Another One 5
Making Tea for My Father 8
Things Your Mother Told You 9
Shut Up 11
Mea Culpa 13
Sisters 14
Thanks for the Genes 16
Misty Morning in Wexford 17
Getting Yourself Sorted 18
Time Warp 20
Glasthule Morning 22
The Weather in Toronto, Winter 2007 23
Dutch Translation 25

PART II

In Praise of Usefulness 29
Eggs 31
Jill Enjoys Her Ponies 33
Touched 34
Visiting an Aunt Who Is Losing Her Memory 35
Signs 37
Adrift in the Boston Public Garden 39
Visitations 40
The Fifth Season Is Mud 41
Happiness 42
The End of the World As We Know It 43

Tonight the Moon is Nothing ... 44
Unfortunate Excitement of the Mind ... 46
What Luki Says … ... 47
Learning by Rote ... 48
Poem in Late April ... 49
Water ... 50

Part III

Fear of Fire ... 53
Wildfire Season ... 55
Lonely Planet ... 56
Time Traveler ... 58
In Which a Day at the Spa Reminds Me of the Asylum
    at Saint-Remy-de-Provence ... 60
A Dream of Order in the Universe ... 61
One Size Fits All ... 63
The Black Door *(An Doras Dorcha)* ... 64
La Rousse ... 66
Alternative Lives ... 67
On The Bus ... 68
What Matter ... 69
Mornings with Coffee ... 70
Learning to Drive, 1978 ... 71
The Emigrant Suite ... 73

Acknowledgements

Some of the poems in this manuscript originally appeared in the following journals:

Boyne Berries (Ireland), "Making Tea for My Father"

Birchsong Anthology: Poetry Centered in Vermont, "Signs," and "Thanks for the Genes"

The Café Review, "Poem in Late April," "Wildfire Season," "Eggs," "The Fear of Fire," and "Shut Up"

Green Mountains Review, "Mea Culpa"

Markings 30 (Scotland), "Sisters"

Nimrod International Journal, "In Praise of Usefulness"

Nimrod International Journal, "Dutch Translation"

Nimrod International Journal, "Things Your Mother Told You," and "The Weather in Toronto, Winter 2007"

Poem City 2012, "Mornings with Coffee"

The Poetry Bus (Ireland), "Learning by Rote," "Visiting an Aunt Who Is Losing Her Memory," "The Black Door (*An Doras Dorcha*)," and "tonight the moon is nothing"

The Salon, "Lonely Planet," and "Getting Yourself Sorted"

Vantage Point, "On The Bus," "In Which a Day at the Spa Reminds Me of the Asylum at Saint-Remy-de-Provence," and "Visitations"

PART 1

Tabula Rasa

I was christened in Westland Row Church
next door to the railway station
so I've always been a bit of a traveler.
Add to that being born on a Thursday
which meant I'd have far to go.

The church was a handy few streets from where I was born
to expedite procurement of eternal life insurance.

With influenza and other figaries on the loose
an infant might well end up on the wrong bus
and go wandering in Limbo like a foreigner.

The marble holywater font was massive
enough to bathe or drown a baby.
But my godmother held me tightly
in voluminous layers of lace and cotton.

I peeped out from under my christening shawl
at the gold and white plaster faces
looking down at me from the ceiling.
Were they cherubs or little children
who had gone before me up to Heaven?

The priest arrived like a bride in white
vestments to cast out my sins
although gluttony was the only one
I'd had any chance to commit
in the seven short days of my life.

Outside the grey stone structures of the city
came to life. Thousands of tweed caps
moved among shadowed alleyways
as coal-smoke belched from duct, pipe and shaft.
Hucksters hawked their meager harvest
as cornerboys keened the mangled names
of newspapers.

They called me Angela
because the Angelus bell was ringing
and Mary for the Mother of Sorrows
who was to become my longtime
traveling companion.

I roared when they rained
cold water on my head, then slept
amid the liturgical lullaby of prayers
and the redolent aroma of incense.

That was a somber place, full of statues
of the crucified Christ
laid out in his mother's arms
like a broken mirror.

I was given martyred saints
for nursery mates, medals
and holy pictures for protection
blood and thorns for my dreams.

Always Room for Another One

In life my relations lived
in one another's ears and arms.
Slept two and three to a bed
in the little pre-War house
on Findlater Street
that had a whitewashed toilet
in the miniscule backyard.
Their numerous cousins
only a stone's throw away
down the cobbled street.

Now even in death
they keep in touch.
Mother's grandparents share
their Glasnevin grave
with a daughter Sarah,
dead at seventeen. Shoved over
for her cousin Annie,
twelve at her death from
tubercular meningitis.

Fifty yards away
Mother's great-grandfather Henry
lies next door to his son Patrick
who joined Julia, his wife,
forty forever since her death.
Squeezed in closer still
for two daughters
Mary and Elizabeth,
both dead by their early teens.

My own grandfather ran away to sea
as a boy, stoked the ship's boiler in a muck-sweat
until pneumonia and the Irish damp
killed him at fifty-eight.

Our mother was christened
Annie Elizabeth Mary Swords
in honor of the maiden aunts
she had never met.

Throughout her life
she never mentioned
the need for peace and quiet
in that jam-packed jumble of relations
whose rubber faces and inside jokes
marked the boundaries
of our known world.

And I never thought it small
when I roller-skated
down the Noggin Hill
to visit the house
where they all grew up
though the tiny hallway
was barely big enough
for one, the livingroom crowded
with people drinking tea,
and the narrow portraits
of Victorian ladies clustered
on the wall near the scullery
with the black gas cooker.

Hadn't she the seaside,
my mother always said,
and the silent sanctity of churches
where her supplications rose
like chimney-smoke
to mingle with soft whispers
of the other sinners
before drifting into
the raftered vault above.

No, she said, we were always
a tribal people. And wouldn't we all
be a long time dead?

Making Tea for My Father

Bring the water to a rolling boil—
there's nothing worse than lukewarm tea.

Take down the metal pot from the shelf—
the one over the gas stove.
It has a few dents but you can't beat it for flavor.
You can throw out those fancy earthenware jobs—
I wouldn't give you thanks for them.

Open the tea-caddy and have a good long sniff.
Since it's only meself and yourself
measure out a heaping spoonful each
and one for the pot.

Don't stint on the tea. That's the sign
of a man so mean he wouldn't spit on you
if you were on fire.

Pour on the water and leave it stew on the gas
for a good ten minutes.

A nice drop of milk and two spoons of sugar
for me if you please. You'll find
a bit of sweet cake in the tin.

Now that will put the red neck on you
and a bit of hair on your chest and no mistake.

Things Your Mother Told You

"Of the various kinds of intelligence, generosity is the first"
—John Surowiecki, Gienka Home from the Ball Bearing Plant (1943)

She could talk the teeth off a saw
or the four legs off a donkey
so there was never any shortage
of uninvited sage advice.

You'd do that while a cat would be chewing a marble.
Meaning would you ever hurry up like a good girl
and stop slouching and wool-gathering
and dreaming your life away?

When you asked how long it would be
until some special occasion
she'd say Tib's Eve, a day
that was neither before nor after Christmas.

And while you were puzzling over that one
she'd tell you that the sun was splitting the stones
and she never saw the likes of you for moping
and you supposed to be so smart.

Meaning wait till your father gets home
and I tell him what you've been up to
while his back was turned. Then we'll see
who's Daddy's little *sleutherer*.

Would your mother send you out
in something that didn't suit you, she'd ask
when she made you wear the pink synthetic topcoat
that had the texture of wet potatoes.

We won't feel it now till the fine weather, she'd say
as soon as the clocks sprang forward
no matter if the heavens had opened
and it was spitting snow or scupping rain.

But when she told you the story of the neighbor
around the corner, how she had fallen on hard times—
a bad marriage and a drinking problem, poor soul—
your head came up like a startled horse.

She had taken the gold ring off her finger
and pressed it into the woman's outstretched palm
not thinking what your father might have said
or whether it was wise

not minding her own ailments
and afflictions, her rheumatism or grief.
Only telling herself for the thousandth time
amn't I the lucky one to have had it so good?

Suddenly you saw her as she had always been—
her generous soul and fine intelligence
under all the talking. And of course
it was too late, you were already gone

and she was still saying goodbye.
But you imagined how she would have blossomed
had they ever let her make her own decisions
had she been lucky enough to have had your life.

Shut Up

was the one utterance she wouldn't allow
although she never shut up herself.

A terrible thing to say to someone
she told us and meant it for once.

Even dragged Our Susan back from
a terrific temper tantrum to take the words

out of her mouth and make her promise
never say them again to a living soul

over her dead body so help me God
or she couldn't call herself a Christian.

If that was the worst she ever heard
her ears would have curled like a Calla lily

at the epithets I uttered after leaving home.
That Christmas when I turned nineteen

in the wilds of Western Ontario
with nothing but a pair of cotton pants

and a fake fur jacket to ward off winter,
those five-cent four-letter words were a bonfire

that burned my tongue and also, I imagined,
my history with its woefully restricted lexicon.

And wasn't I surprised when no one threatened
to burn me at the stake or hang me

in a cage from the spire of Munster Cathedral
to sputter my blasphemies to the indifferent skies

as they did the loose-lipped Albigensian heretics
who couldn't shut up to save their lives.

Mea Culpa

"My only regret is that I wasn't born somebody else."
—Woody Allen

Sorry I'm late, you whisper
as you slip into the room
with your breath in your fist.

Sorry, sorry, I'm sorry you mumble
as you step over knees, ankles
shopping bags to reach your seat.

The Irish are forever saying sorry.

Sorry we say when some stranger
bumps into us on the street
sends our parcels flying.

He's a sorry-looking article
we say of the wet dog, drunken neighbor
tight-lipped civil servant.

For all the sins of my past life
and those I haven't yet committed
I am truly and irrefutably sorry.

Sorry to interrupt, sorry to have to tell you
sorry for your troubles, trials and tribulations
sorry for living.

Stop apologizing, your sister-in-law keeps telling you
not realizing that self-deprecation is your Siamese twin
and not even surgery could separate you now.

Say you're sorry, we tell our children
when we catch them acting the maggot.
Or I'll give you something to be sorry about.

Sisters

We were supposed to call them Mother
those consecrated brides of Christ
who wore virginity like a virtue
profession rings on their wedding fingers
making us wonder what they thought
of our own mothers safe at home
presumably enjoying carefree, sinful lives
although my mother seemed as holy
and her life anything but free.

I liked Mother Dolores best, her country accent
and her kindness, the shadow of a mustache
on her upper lip. She said that what we didn't know
would fill libraries, and I could picture
shelves upon shelves of dusty dictionaries
documenting my abysmal ignorance
that stretched toward a distant vanishing point.

Mother Patrick was tiny, furious
a hummingbird in massive headdress
who hurled herself at us, dagger beak disclosing
mismatched shoes, our shortened gymslips, lost berets.

Mother Stephen was the quiet one, save for the rattle
of the rosary beads against her stiff blue tunic
her bashfulness betrayed by the pink flushed skin
against her white bandeau.

One autumn we returned to school
to learn the Order's headquarters in Cluny
had handed down an edict. No more
enormous coifs and coronets and no more Mothers.

Instead we were to call these shrunken-headed females
Sister, although we still knew nothing of their lives
what they wore under their medieval habits
if their heads were shaved or if they missed
their real sisters, now they shared an invisible husband
who was also, inexplicably, their Father.

Thanks for the Genes

Father, it's time I thanked you for
this slender body, its quick metabolism
its uncanny knack for fighting off infection
its tolerant digestive tract
accommodating as an ash-pit.

I didn't inherit your taste for potatoes
boiled in their jackets
peppery turnips fried on the pan
or two spoons of sugar in your tea.
But thanks to you I can eat
almost anything without remorse.

Forget the delicate fingers, polished nails.
My hands look like yours after a day in the garden
pruning roses and shoveling manure.
Workman's hands, thick fingers
veins standing out like the contour lines
on a topographic map of Ireland.

This face you gave me was a tough one
to love, especially now it's turning Cubist
in the mirror, full of jagged planes
and jutting angles, shifting tectonic plates.
Though it does have character
I'll grant you that.

I'm still wrestling with your dagger's looks
your suspicious nature, your moody brooding.
Like Jewelweed, invasive Touch-Me-Not,
that sneaks surreptitiously into the flower-bed
just when you think you finally stamped it out.

Misty Morning in Wexford

for John

Brambly hedgerows against a grey sky
the trees like old ghosts in the distance
disfigured by wind unceasing off the sea.
My brother and I engrossed, listening
to the soundtrack of our teens—
a Stax/Volt-Motown-Van Morrison-via-Mississippi
Delta-Talkin'-Bout My-Generation compilation
that conjures sweaty tennis club dances
pounding rhythms, slow sets and furtive kisses
the suntanned glow of our Irish skins
in the false romance of ultraviolet light.

Here in the house my brother designed
where deep terracotta and warm yellow shadows
linger over rich wood doors, I think
of our father's restrained pastel palette—
the easy-to-clean peach walls and flowered wallpapers
that (like his hard work and expertise) never varied.
Turn off that damn noise, he used to say
when Procol Harum played *A Whiter Shade of Pale*
or the Stones sang *Paint It Black* on the pirate station.
And later how my brother's new-found tastes
took on the very tint of mutiny.

Getting Yourself Sorted

When you were young, his shadow filled the front door
hers the kitchen. You studied them like an explorer
poring over the cartography of a new continent.

Until the day the tinker girl appeared on the doorstep
a wisp of red hair escaping from her shawl
a swaddled infant underneath her oxter.

Go in now, love, like a good girl, she commanded you.
Ask your Mammy for a sup of milk for the baby
and I'll say a prayer that a nice man will marry you.

You looked at yourself in your blue school gymslip
gawky as a light-deprived houseplant
then fled back to your books and pencils

terrified at the prospect of some drunken lout
landing you with a baby and you
still only a child yourself.

Fast-forward then to adolescence when you haunted
all the pubs in Dublin, discussing the deficiencies
of those gigantic obstacles, your parents

their stony silences, implacable refusal to let you
grow up, make your own mistakes
leave home, ruin your own life.

A few years later you had hacked the hawsers
to unmoor yourself. The baby perpetually parked
on your hip like a big moon straddling the horizon

as you paddled, frightened, gulping air
but still afloat in your leaky craft, heading towards
that faraway country some called adulthood.

Luckily for you your life cracked up, rebalanced.
Your parents grew smaller with age. Your mother
a bright fly-catcher, dashing out for the morning messages.

Your father a mere sparrow, full of songs and sweetness.
By then you were relieved to discover your place
among the rocks and trees, the other animals.

The way a photographer might shoot your portrait
next to a giant redwood, everything arranged
to indicate a three-dimensional perspective.

Time Warp

"All the people we used to know/they're an illusion to me now."
—Bob Dylan, Tangled Up In Blue

A woman's voice on the telephone
someone I haven't seen in forty years.
She has three children, all married

a husband, a house in West Cork
another in South Dublin.
I try to imagine a girl with brown curly hair

a blue school uniform, a musical laugh
sitting in front of me in the classroom.
I liked her then but who has she become?

A gaggle of women in the restaurant
their heads together over the tea and cakes
babies snoozing in their strollers

could be the girls I knew at school
if I etch-a-sketch three decades to their faces.
But I can't envision Ailish, Grainne, Eileen.

Keep overlooking how I've aged
since leaving Ireland, not this time
on a winged horse but on an Airbus

bound for the Land of Youth.
Like Oisin I longed to return, forgetting
that all would be unfamiliar.

Except the voices, distinctive as fingerprints
the unchanging sea crashing against grey granite
collecting its breath as the tide recedes.

And the gulls frozen like figures in a medieval fresco
continuing their ancient tug-of-war
over the stinking remains of fish.

Glasthule Morning

for Bernadette

Silver traceries of snails around the cat's dish.
A checkered magpie flashes in to steal a morsel.
A flock of sparrows natter in the privet hedge—
even the shrubbery is talking.

The Weather in Toronto, Winter 2007

What part of Canada are ye from
the security guard in Belfast asks politely
as we step out of the car at the college gate.

Vermont, I say, in the U.S. But I'm Irish
born and raised, I hasten to add, as I ladle out
an extra dollop of my Dublin accent.

But it says here ye are Canadian, he insists
tapping his finger on his official memo.
Later someone mentions a grand wee holiday

in Niagara Falls, a daughter in Alberta
a weather bulletin that says it's snowing in Toronto.
When they ask what took you out to Canada

in the first place I don't bother to defend myself
shamed by the name of my old neighborhood
though it's three decades since I left home

and no one remembers the seedy history of my street
now the houses have changed hands
and people have money in their pockets.

Next day our driver gives us "the terror tour"
of Belfast—the Europa Hotel bombed 37 times
the train station rebuilt from scratch.

Here's where the minister was shot. Here's the corner
where I saw a man lying dead in a pool of blood.
Nothing to worry about now. Not a wee bother.

Everyone here is happy to forget that history
ever happened. So why am I still lugging mine around
as if it was written on my forehead

like the mark of Cain or a terrorist slogan
dripping red paint down a rickety barricade—
part feeble fortification, part belligerent defense.

Dutch Translation

A painting is nothing but daubs on canvas.
A photo—only a puppet theater
play of light and shadow.
A poem—black scratches on paper
like rows of stitches on a quilt of snow.

But the ladies in the National Gallery
crowd closer, as though Vermeer's
domestic interior were a showhouse
To Let in a Dublin suburb, a place
they might imagine as their own.

Coffee in the morning with *The Irish Times,*
the sheen of rain on a slate roof.
Light entering through net curtains,
obsidian glimmer of a leather sofa.
Persian rug, pearl earring.

PART II

In Praise of Usefulness

The long spoon hammered
from a single hunk of metal
by my friend the blacksmith
hangs from a hook on our kitchen wall.
Testament to his friendship
which is solid too
and plainspoken, permanent.

Nearby the bowl my neighbor culled
from the red dirt of Northern Vermont
his sure hands seducing curves
from common clay.

By the woodstove the four-pronged
metal fork my father fashioned
to protect our hands and faces
when we toasted bread
at the open fire for tea.

Mother loved the utility of kitchen gadgets
the tiny wires that sliced a hardboiled egg
into identical subdivisions.
The plastic rainhat folded lengthwise
like a map, whisked from her handbag
to protect an ephemeral perm.

The ingenuity of ordinary things
delighted her. Yet she underestimated
usefulness as if it was only
beauty's poor relation.

If you can't be ornamental
then be useful, she instructed
not thinking how her words
would twist my vision, shape
my unfolding image of myself.

But see this vessel, I want to tell her.
This cup that holds my sacramental
morning coffee. How it fits my palm.
Its roundness like a full belly.
The dark blue of its glaze.
The rough comfort of its lip.

Eggs

Lately I've been thinking
about eggs,
their perfect shape,
their shells smooth
as an infant's footsole,
seamless as a stone.
Eggs are independent,
self-contained,
the way I'd like
my life to be,
except that I keep
thinking of it
as an egg-and-spoon race
in which I'm dashing blindly forward,
trying to hold my spoon steady
so as not to drop the baby
on his fragile skull,
his fontanelle still beating.
There was a man
in my old neighborhood
whose skull had been cracked
like an egg,
then glued together
just enough
to let him follow directions,
do what his mother told him,
walk furiously around
the Five Sister streets all day
and try not to frighten
small children.
I'd like everything to be orderly,

perfectly balanced
as an egg.
But I keep hearing
that distant tapping
getting louder, the sound
of an insistent beak
that won't give up
until it has broken
through.

Jill Enjoys Her Ponies

With apologies to Ruby Ferguson, author of Black Boy,
Jill Enjoys Her Ponies, and other books for girls.

Do you ever think about Samson & Delilah
I ask my hairdresser. I mean, does it ever occur to you
that all my strength may have gone into my hair
and I'll end up a well-groomed shadow of my former self?

She raises a penciled eyebrow, says she's never heard of Samson
or his scissors-happy girlfriend. That my hair will grow again
and it's time I stopped looking like an overgrown schoolgirl.

She has never been marched to the cinema by nuns
to watch *The Greatest Story Ever Told*, or wept in terror
when the subjugated strongman tore the marble pillars down
in a final burst of Old Testament rage.

My students likewise wouldn't know a parable from
a peacock feather, a Biblical allusion from the jawbone of an ass.
The faintly audible soundtrack of their inner lives
buzzes like the whirring of a thousand maddened bees.

Back to my hair as it falls in unwanted clumps on the salon floor.
How I used to bathe it like a newborn in bowls of rosemary
and chamomile. Plaster it with egg-yolks and mayonnaise
as if it was a pony I was primping for the big gymkhana

which was the closest I would ever get to the horsey-Irish
with their hard-hats and jodhpurs that some Americans
liked to imagine was my mess of pottage
my hereditary social milieu.

Touched

for Mary

I was touched that you held my hand in the car
before we said goodbye, my sister says shyly
over the telephone after returning home.
And I was touched when she linked my arm
as we walked along the seafront promenade.
Both of us touched and needing to be touched.

A moment when we abandoned armor
laid down our weapons as if they were no more
than bamboo curtains, paper walls.
The way the sunlight threw its weight around
this morning, elbowing dark clouds aside
to shine through fitfully (as it always does in Ireland)

which makes you love its cameo appearances
walk-on parts, a burst of warmth after rain.

Visiting an Aunt
Who Is Losing Her Memory

And which side of the Atlantic are you on
this time, she asks when I telephone to say
I'm coming over. We laugh at the old joke
both of us having switched places decades since.
Her New England girlhood long gone
she still remembers hot summer days in Maine
the crisp midwinters of Massachusetts.

My Dublin accent is a hybrid now, neither one thing
nor another. She has never stopped being American
though her knitted cardigans and homemade dresses
with their matching purses put her closer
to the Amish matrons of Central Pennsylvania
than the Boston Brahmin ladies of her day.

It's wet October weather in South Dublin
and I haven't been warm since I left Vermont.
Leaves clog the gutters along the seafront
where gulls root for food in rotting seaweed.

Outside her kitchen window small birds swarm
around the seed-feeder. I remember my wedding
in this house, the hall lined with expensive gifts
a dowry I could not provide myself.

How she taught me to bake yeast bread, raising
the seven weekly loaves in a plastic baby bath.
Dispensed jamjars of her homemade yogurt
to the neighborhood's young mothers
as if coagulated milk contained a remedy
that could save them from despair.

We chat on, sipping tea, as she pries open
all the doors of her memory to peer inside.
Kisses me when I leave. You'll be back
won't you, she asks hopefully. Next day
her daughter says she knew she'd had a visitor—
couldn't remember who it was.

Signs

Even after I got over all religion
abandoned the very idea of an *Afterlife*
I kept looking for a sign, some
directional signal that would indicate
stay or go, this man or the other.

Like an amputee's limb that continues
to agitatate after being severed
I wanted answers that were clear
unequivocal. A mathematical equation
a cardinal number. The answer, it turned out

was more like one of those infuriating
mystery novels where you get to choose
which door your poor protagonist
will open as he fumbles for
the light switch in the dark.

I've never found a sign that wasn't wish-
fulfillment, a mock-up of my own creation.
Like last night driving home I found myself
meandering down a road I'd never seen before.
I had no idea which direction I should take

and for a while I drove as if lifted out of time
cut off from the current of my own existence
no tether tying me to either end.
Exhilarating really to feel so free.
And the sunset, which I hardly ever notice

was spectacular, all reds and purples
deepening to twilight. I passed two horses
cropping late October grass by the roadside
the pond behind them a cup of the light
that tipped their manes and tails with mercury.

But I know better than to call
that luminous ploy a portent, a sign.
I've always wondered if my real life
was being lived by some *doppelganger*
on another dimension of Google.com.

Hang out your shingle, they used to say
and mine might well read *Under Construction
Come Back Later, Closed for Repairs.*

Adrift in the Boston Public Garden

Here comes a woman crossing the street
a Pekinese slung like a spoiled infant
in a faux leopardskin bag across her breasts.

Today strangers are preferable to family
with their tongues like acupuncture needles
manipulating the meridians of pain.

In the storefront window on Newbury Street
stand hundreds of Singer sewing machines
their black cylindrical bodies

like ghosts of their former operatives
who toiled over trousers and topcoats
in windowless rooms above the street.

Amassed inside the fashionable gloom
repose piles of mud-colored sweaters
distressed leather boots, pre-ravaged bluejeans

any one of them worth more than
the weekly rent for a spare alcove
in one of Boston's congested tenements.

Why do cities always make a Puritan of me?
I'm becoming old—no desire to consume anything.
I think of my home and the frog-pond

the beautiful Rose-breasted Grosbeak
his strawberry-stained shirtfront
his magnanimous liquid song.

Visitations

The way that deer materialize
out of nowhere in the yard at dusk
never ceases to amaze me.

As if some apparition of the Virgin
suddenly appeared and asked
my help to save the world.

But these shy creatures from
a parallel universe make no demands
ask nothing of us but our silence.

Late afternoon light pours over
their soft brown backs. Their long ears
twitch like radio antennae.

We never know when they will appear
to traverse our rocky hillside, step lightly
on their delicate unhesitating hooves.

And when I turn my head they pass
out of sight into the trees, called by
the wind's otherworldly music.

The Fifth Season Is Mud

Today the road relaxes, unclenching itself
like a pair of tired shoulders.

Snow slides off the roof in great wet corrugated sheets
drips onto the veined leaves of the variegated hosta
so slowly that the ear quivers, swiveling
towards the next inevitable drop.

Yesterday the trees stood rigid in their icy overcoats.
Today they are sagging, slumping, letting go.

Before I came to the country
I did not know that winter ebbed and flowed
that trees could break in a high wind.
That every creature in nest, cleft or den
from the mild brown spider
hidden in the lampshade
safe as a mouse in a malt-heap
to the rapacious woodchuck
gorging the first green shoots of basil
had found, if not a purpose
then at least a place.

Happiness

Who knew it would be so simple
after all those years of insufficient
money, insufficient love.

The dread of mornings, chance encounters
crossing the street to avoid hello
hiding upstairs when the doorbell rang.

Believing it was the end of the world
when it hadn't yet begun.

I've had to learn to set aside the fear
of God's mean-spirited retaliation
walk into the garden with a wooden bowl
pinch back the basil for its clove aroma
pull the young green lettuce leaves
the golden sage, the feathery dill weed.

I've had to forgive myself for crawling
slow as a timid tortoise towards maturity
forgive my body for galloping through time
like a startled racehorse, forgive my face
for always giving me away.

Risk opening the screen door.
Inviting summer to come in.

The End of the World As We Know It

Some days I sense the vast commotion
of the natural world. Detect the wriggle
of the lowly worm aerating soil.

The myopic mole's quick flippers
swimming underneath the surface of the garden
widening ripples appearing in his wake.

Hear the frantic heartbeat of the fieldmouse
as the horned owl's head swivels full circle
and its huge golden eye fixes its prey like a photograph.

A flutter of wings and there like a discord
is the scrape of the brown-headed cowbird's beak
nudging the dove's egg over the side of the nest.

It's always the end of the world for someone.

Tonight the Moon is Nothing

but a faint circle in the frigid sky.
The night brittle as glass.
Rumors of snow on the radio.

This morning all seemed clear—
the dim path you followed
throughout your life revealed—
though none of it was certain at the time.
Not the destination or the path itself
or even the possibility that it might
have been a path at all.

The only thing you knew was to remain
resistant as wax on a piece of ragged cloth.
Refuse to register the pattern
proscribed by priest or prophet.

Then a series of disasters followed
like wide-spaced stepping-stones
in a roiling stream.
Each one the only option
and a poor one at that.
No way to turn back
though you considered it many times.

What was it that propelled you forward?
Not wisdom surely
when you borrowed money to go to school
or took a ruinous pay-cut to study poetry.
You almost laughed aloud
that time a student talked of living
'an intentional life.'

But in this moment's moonlit clarity
it looks as if your own life was laid out
flat as a board-game—
straight shot to the finish line.
Always the ladder
never the snake.

Unfortunate Excitement of the Mind

Title of a painting by Alois Bilek, Czech abstract painter, 1913–1961

Snooping around the Art Institute of Chicago
I saw a teacher stop before Seurat's
A Sunday on La Grande Jatte.

It's all made of dots, she whispered
to the children gathered solemnly around her.
Just little squiggly dots.

And they stood there absorbing Pointillism
like their first taste of mango or persimmon.
Slippery sweetness.
A new sensation on the tongue.
Wrinkling their noses. Considering.
Opening their mouths for more.

I used to take my son for walks
when he was young, still low to the ground.
We sifted leaves, searching for conkers, stones.
Ate pretend sandwiches made of
air and imagination.

Then I repented all the moments
I had devoured like empty calories.
The way vast flocks of students huddle close
their earbuds dangling like rabbinical sidecurls
each one sequestered in a private music.

Or the couple in the restaurant
intently pressing buttons on their smartphones
instead of pressing one another's flesh
which takes another kind of smarts.

What Luki Says...

I'm going to be four all day.
What does time mean?

I don't think I want to grow up
because I won't like mud
and I'll have to do
a hundred gallons of homework.

Why can't a vacuum cleaner
suck out cancer germs?

How can someone cry
if she doesn't have eyes?

Where is the bottom of space?

I think I'll eat mango
for the rest of my life.

Learning by Rote

Luki at six is learning the names of dinosaurs—
Giganotosaurus, Titanosaurus, Pteranodon.
He marvels at their massive jaws, their claws

and teeth, their appetite for widespread mayhem.
Marvels too at my ignorance of prehistory
science, anatomy, almost everything.

At six I had to memorize the Maynooth Catechism,
learn words like *sepulcher, crucifixion, calumniate*.
Recite the litany of the seven deadly sins

seven sacraments, seven gifts of the Holy Ghost.
Cudgel my conscience to deduce
the destructive consequences of my crimes.

Luki prefers the Cretaceous to the Jurassic period.
I liked the names of obscure saints
who were fed to lions in the Coliseum.

He peoples new planets with Lego, colored pencils, paper.
I mapped angelic choirs of Seraphim and Cherubim
Thrones and Dominions, Virtues, Powers

and Principalities, laying up for myself treasures in heaven.
Both of us true believers in what we are told—
spectacular vertebrates, stupefying monsters, flying saints.

Poem in Late April

Just before *The Great Disappointment*
when the Elect could still believe
they had been singled out for salvation.

Just before the trees began flinging themselves
into blossom, serving up dollops of raspberry sherbet
and peppermint stick with clotted cream.

Just before you could remember
being still too young to imagine
what it felt like to be old.

You walked around gawking upwards
at each delectable concoction
tasting possibility on the breeze.

You were riding the upswing of the seesaw
thrust up so high and wild you forgot about
lever and fulcrum, the ripening and the falling-off.

Just before the month your mother said
was all for you. A gift so lovely it would take you
all your life to take it in.

Water

Yesterday we turned on the taps
in the kitchen. A brief trickle, then nothing.
Not frozen pipes, we whispered anxiously.
A burst main up the road, the papers said.
No worries. Then this morning water
gushing forth like the Pierian Spring
or blushful Hippocrene. The shower-head
a giant sunflower bending tenderly over me
as I stood there letting the water cascade
over shoulders, breasts and buttocks.
I relished the luscious soap, costly shampoo
the perfumes of the Orient, even a loofah
to scourge away my sins of self-indulgence.
I thought of the California drought
a rainless winter, vast deserts of Sahara
Mojave, Kalahari. Poor people in villages
across the world, their unwashed bodies
bare feet tramping arid dusty roads
their wells run dry, no drinking water
let alone this heavenly deluge.

What could I do but savor
each incalculable drop?

PART III

Fear of Fire

I knew a woman once who burned hot
as a sleeping volcano. If you got too close to her
she'd blow, smash dishes. One time
an entire casserole on her way to a potluck picnic.
I've always feared that kind of red-hot wrath
its blindness and its strength.

I like a decorous argument with rules
both parties can respect. Like no
backhanded slices, no crossing the net
into the opponent's court.
Just Forty-Love and a handshake.

But there's this man I know. Fights dirty.
Gets his teeth in and won't let go.
His rage flies up like a prairie fire
and there's nowhere to hide
in all that vast expanse
where the huge empty sky
hitches up to the horizon.

I think of him on a day like this
when arctic air seeps under the fabric snake
wedged in the doorframe
and the fire is both master and menace.

When the thermometer on the woodstove
dips down low, I open the side door warily
brandishing the poker like a circus lion-tamer
with a whip and chair.

But at five hundred degrees the stove
begins to speak in its creaky cast-iron voice
warning that soon the flames will burst
from their metal prison to devour the house.

I leap to grab the smooth brass handle
of the fire spanner, tighten the dials
at front and sides to choke off oxygen
throttle the inferno's mad intent.

My grandfather knew the nature of the beast.
A stoker on a ship, he shoveled coal
into an open furnace door
sweat darkening his dirty singlet
his ginger moustache reddening in the light.

Later in the clammy cold of an Irish winter
he took a chill that became pneumonia
and caught his death in a dull hospital
full of damp walls and empty grates.

When this man I know flares up
I gather all my words and fling them
willy-nilly like thimbles full of water
at a blazing house.

Don't touch me, says the stove-top,
boiling kettle, frying pan. Stop
adding tinder to the flames.

Wildfire Season

for Jane

I see you on the concrete streets
of East Liverpool, Ohio
that industrial Crockery City where you were born.
Your red hair like the berries of a Mountain Ash
setting fire to a gray morning.

Oh Jane, fires are burning
in the Little Bear, New Mexico
in Skull Creek, Wyoming
all over your beloved Montana.

Wind-driven, unpredictable
charring acres in an hour
they obscure the sun at midday
sometimes jump containment lines
leave burn scars on the land pink as singed flesh—
the indelible mark of a sacrament
that obliterates the past.

Oh Jane, your body was up for anything
before sickness started running through you
like a wildfire. Some people escaped
left you to shift for yourself.

Now firefighters have learned to get out of the way
allow those conflagrations to do
their disinfecting work. Eradicate
thick canopies, brushy undergrowth.
Permit sunlight to reach the forest floor.

Maybe the rains will come soon.
Maybe a miracle will happen.
Maybe you can just let it burn.

Lonely Planet

"Odors that the smolts experience during this time of heightened sensitivity are stored in the brain and become important direction-finding cues years later, when adults attempt to return to their home streams."
—*The Scientific American.*

I am a fish
the Iraqi man on NPR says quietly
and Baghdad is my sea.
If I do not return to it
I will die.

He is going back to the place
where he watched aghast
as three teenage boys
pulled a man from a car
and shot him in the head
the dark blood seeping down
the narrow street like a scandal.

The place where an old woman
crossing the road to buy bread
her garments billowing
like a ship with black sails
was blown to pieces
by a suicide bomber
who could not bear
to wait his turn at death
but had to rig the race
win by a photo finish
prove himself worthy
of a place in paradise.

Homesick for months
the Iraqi man is happy
now he has made up his mind
to return to the place
where he hopes to be buried
next to his wife, his parents.

The place where his family gathers
to celebrate births and birthdays
eat *fattoush, tabbouleh, hummus*
remark on the miracle
of merely being alive.

Not like his American colleague
who left his wife for another woman
and now finds himself in a foreign country
missing his passport, visa, compass

the Iraqi man no longer wonders
if his homing instinct represents
fidelity or fiction.

Lucky to be a fish
that loves its bowl.

Time Traveler

In memory of Rose Levin, 1909-2012

Rose, at one-hundred-and-two, tells her caregiver
she is pregnant. Next day she breaks the news
that she is getting married. The caregiver
a Russian woman with muscular arms and a voice
full-bodied as borscht, raises her eyebrows.
A little backwards, nu?

But Rose only smiles, retreating in time
her snowy hair already darkening on the pillow.
Today she's Mrs. Levin, young mother in Brooklyn.
Was it only yesterday she passed herself off
as dark-eyed Rose Galagano to get a job?

Light filters in through the slatted blinds
gilding the forest of photo frames, glinting off
the protective plastic cover of the armchair.

What was she saving it for?
The mahjong players have vanished
their ornate tiles tucked away in their box on the bureau
the hum of apartment-building gossip hushed
almost to a whisper.

Others glide in and out of the old apartment—
number-two-H-as-in-Harry, she always said.
Sometimes it's Ben, her husband, long dead
but always a gentleman in his well-pressed suit.
Sometimes her sister Doris who lives
a few blocks over on King's Highway.

Sometimes she surfaces from the long sleep
that is now her life to gaze at this strange new world
she is about to leave. Time is simply
a fourth dimension, and her elegant machine
with its intricate buttons and silk upholstery
is almost ready for take-off.

Will she get as far as Broome Street
or Ellis Island, maybe even Minsk
before the trip is done?

In Which a Day at the Spa Reminds Me of the Asylum at Saint-Remy-de-Provence

for Maveret

We loiter in the spa's hushed sanctuary
amid the ferns and folderol
like hopeful penitents
in white robes and plastic sandals
waiting to hear our names
discreetly called for *treatment*.

Masquerading as a pair of well-heeled wives
with legs long as the pedigrees
of pampered house-pets
we are the utter monkey's uncle
the genuine cat's pajamas.

Later strolling in the spa's walled garden
among the culinary herbs and flowers
I cannot help but think
of Vincent and his brother Theo
walking arm-in-arm around the asylum
at Saint-Rémy-de-Provence.

Was this what tortured him, I wonder—
this absurd disparity between
the pampered and the paupers?

Still it's hard to stop my mouth
from watering at the prospect
of the body butter, rose petals and pomegranate polish
some faceless staff person will slather on our skins
preparing us to act like happy lunatics
when visiting hour rolls round.

A Dream of Order
in the Universe

Carl Linnaeus (1707–1778) was a Swedish botanist, physician, and zoologist, who laid the foundations for the modern scheme of binomial nomenclature.

Marcia's hormones keep her up all night
dancing jigs around the bedroom, then
fanning themselves on the sidelines
before joining the next maniacal jamboree.

One doctor recommends a week
of estrogen, a second says progesterone.
Don't touch those synthetic hormones,
a third advises. And whatever you do

try to hang on to your uterus as long as you can.
You're still juicy, a friend squawks
clawing a tanned bicep, tugging a fat earlobe.

But not for long. Soon you'll become
invisible. Men will look clear through you
and you'll pinch yourself to see if you still exist.

Online, Denise is more positive
speaks of living in a hormonal household
her careful exercise plan, her protein diet.

Bonnie recalls her hysterectomy
then her first hot flash, which Pam
insists on calling a *power surge*.

Corinne says her Chinese fan is indispensable
for sudden heatwaves, occasional tsunamis
and other menstrual maladies.

As for me, I'm placing my faith in Black Cohosh
Evening Primrose, Royal Jelly
in honor of Linnaeus and his love of flowers
his dream of order in the universe.

One Size Fits All

In the ladies' underwear shop I paw
through piles of padded, push-up, polka-dotted
wired and wireless contraptions
in search of the smallest size.

There's the Wonderbra with its intricate
ropes and pulleys. The Sportsbra—first cousin
to the whalebone corset. The Jogbra—
an Ace bandage for minimizing bounce.

As if I ever needed minimizing.

I'm sure the shop assistant has a look of pity
in her eyes. I want to ask her if she knows
what it was like to be fifteen and to wonder
why your chest was flat as a skillet
while your mother's flesh oozed over its lacy restraints
like a soft dough newly risen.

The assistant measures me expertly
and delivers her verdict—size thirty-six, double-A cup.
We'll have to order one for you, she says
appraising my insufficient torso.

Double-A, the scarlet letter.

I imagine poor Hester Prynne
condemned to wear her shameful cup size on her chest
as punishment for Pearl's existence.

We're interrupted by a phone-call—
someone needs size H but double-D
is as far as they go. Another special order
to add chagrin to my sin of self-regard.

At home I reveal my digital destiny
to my husband. She's wrong, he says stoutly.
You're not a double-A.
These hands don't lie!

The Black Door *(An Doras Dorcha)*

Years later now she says she loves
her life, her friends, her travels.
Sometimes riding her bicycle in the rain
she is overtaken by a sudden gush of joy.

But when he died she said it wasn't
as if she had lost a part of herself.
More like losing her whole body
except for a small part—
a hand maybe.

She used to imagine it lying forlornly
on the kitchen floor. Didn't know
if she could ever grow back the rest.
And for a long time didn't care.
Was gone missing.

Knew enough to ignore those who try
to manage grief by limiting its length.
Six months, a year, then time is up.
Time to be getting on with it.
Get out of those widow's weeds.
Wear something cheerful, for god's sake.

Even her daughter had had enough.
Said it wasn't fair, as if she had lost
both parents instead of one.

Had always been a swimmer
salt in her mad red hair. The old bathing-suit
baggy but still serviceable enough
for a morning dip. Down the lane
to the Martello tower.

Down into the weightless dark
to knock on the Black Door.
Waited admittance, then had to
back away, surface like any living thing
ascending toward the light.

La Rousse

for Olga

It's a wig, you know, she tells me,
though I hadn't realized.

After the convent she swore
she'd never cover her head again.

Rode her bicycle sans helmet.
Wouldn't carry an umbrella for diamonds.

La Belle Rousse, the Frenchwoman whispered
to her companion in the restaurant.
Typical of the Irish.

Then chemotherapy trumped religion—
a pound of flesh the bargain basement price.

But with that mop of corkscrewed curls
curtailed, she could not recognize
her own shadow on the pavement.

Now the false extension of her rowdy locks
is like a foster-child whose presence
prompts miraculous conception.

That manufactured mane is wilder
redder, truer than her old cropped self
reduced, pretending to be brave.

Alternative Lives

Over drinks in the wine bar he talks of books
ideas, his top ten favorite films, the music
that got him through the hard parts of his life.

You are busy reading body language
noting the spark of interest in his eyes.
Time to mention your husband at home

at this very moment probably crooning
to the cat, whistling a duet with a phoebe
urging his flowers on to bloom.

And it's as if an invisible hand has drawn
a blackout blind between you
and the man across the table.

You watch the light fade out of his eyes
like the sun disappearing
over the distant Adirondacks

all that rosy glow gathering in the storefront
windows, then dying as the evening retracts
leaving the lake in darkness.

Later you are driving home along the river road.
Windows rolled down to catch the clamor
of spring peepers in a teeming pond.

Thinking again of his eyes, their sudden
flecks of green like weeds in pond-water
bog-light at dusk.

A warning not to venture in too far
or swim out beyond your depth.

On The Bus

The road is a jeweled ribbon of asphalt
from which the snow has melted
under the weight of a thousand cars.

On either side loom black and white
slashes of granite rock face. Dark tree limbs
raised as if in anger against the dazzling sky.

What loneliness must lie within
the tidy farmhouses, the white steepled churches
the silver silos straggling the hills.

This morning at the station he said the pain
was like a razorblade twisting inside him.
Pain of lost children, lost chances.

A string of chilly wives who never touched
except when necessary. And his own needs
fading further with each successive child.

You know there are other versions of the story
other assessments of the past. But this is not *Rashomon*
and you no stainless arbiter of truth.

From the window of the bus a skein of ponies
in a pasture. Their blankets like the rough clothes
of peasants in a Brueghel painting.

And the jagged stubble in the cornfield
marching in straight lines towards the horizon.
Small. Impersonal. Relentless.

What Matter

I watch you naked in a dream
surprised to see you balancing
on the parallel bars like any
careless gymnast, your powerful arms
a buttress for your elegant torso.

Now a single handstand, legs akimbo
like Leonardo's *Vitruvian Man*
suspended in a circle, doomed
to ride the wheel of fortune
endlessly.

Except that in this dream
nothing holds you down.
You dance in air, muscular
yet supple as a string.

Voyeur that I am, I admire
the beauty of your smooth
extremities, the texture
of your skin's thick certainty.

What matter that I wake and you are
seventy, fully dressed and foostering
over coffee in the kitchen
your copper-colored beard
three-quarters salt.

Mornings with Coffee

You always bring it in the small blue cup
that fits my hand, its smooth full lip
familiar, comforting.

The coffee strong and black. A ritual
perfected. No unnecessary gestures
no ripple on the pond of morning.

Once in another life, my silence masked
the racket of the war inside my head.
Made mockery of domesticity, devotion.

And even now most days I fail to love
the life I never meant to have.
Distracted by delusions that the world

is celebrating elsewhere, kicking up
its heels, shaking out its tail-feathers
getting on famously without me.

Comes a moment such as this
when a little grace kicks in
and there is just this pleasure—

the wisdom of our hands.
No thinking.

Learning to Drive, 1978

I gripped the steering-wheel white-knuckled
muttering Catholic prayers and aspirations
while the Milton high school driving instructor
murmured encouragement and madly pressed
the emergency pedal.

The child sang the *clutch-and-brake* song
from the back seat. Mother
just off the boat from Ireland
clucked clichés while I contemplated
our mutual dismemberment.

I passed the driving test in a dream,
still too terrified to drive. One night
ditched my car, trudged three miles home in snow,
woke whimpering from visions of cars careening downhill,
me in the driver's seat pumping unresponsive brakes,
the wheel a giant rubber-band
twisting helplessly in my hands.

I imagined accidents at every turn,
wheels coming undone, the gas tank
in my old Ford Pinto exploding,
the crazed driver on the Garden State Parkway
hot on my tail, muttering obscenities.

I've logged thousands of miles since then,
hauling my fragile bones around
in one sardine tin or another.

Every day I don imaginary blinkers,
quiet the part of me that wants to bolt like *Barbaro*,
nostrils flaring, hooves clacking
down the exit ramp to leap the guard-rail
into the nearest pasture.

No, I tell myself. Remember.
Zen driving. You are the Buddha
behind the wheel. Not just a renegade racehorse
on the New Jersey turnpike—
that cacophonous steel inferno.

The Emigrant Suite

"O, my America! my new-found-land"
John Donne, Elegy XX, To His Mistress Going to Bed

O my America, my land of contradictions!
You never opened a door without closing
a window. At home where they never heard
of window screens, the bluebottles bellied
up to the cakes behind the bakery glass
while the soft rain scuttered down unceasing.

Here there's lovely weather to be sure.
But the deer flies and mosquitoes
would eat you without salt.
Acres of trees stretch away so still and self-contained.
Idyllic lakes and pristine ponds that put me in mind
of the Irish Sea and the salty mouthfuls I gulped
while my teeth chattered, lips turned blue,
and the grownups huddled on the beach
drinking pots of scalding tea from the huckster's shop
trying to stay warm.

America, I'm grateful for all you've done
but I crossed my fingers at the naturalization ceremony
when the judge said you're all Americans now
not Turks or Greeks, Armenians or Lithuanians.
No, you're just like us, homogenous as milk.

The other night in the pub an Irish fellow
leaned over and asked me in a whisper—
Are you like me that you only buy
a half pint of milk because you think
maybe you'll be gone home
before you get a chance to drink it?

www.ingramcontent.com/pod-product-compliance
Lightning Source LLC
Chambersburg PA
CBHW071538080526
44588CB00011B/1713